Fleur A Furry Tail

Saving one dog will not change the world, but for one little dog, the world changed forever

Written by Wendy Morris

Follow Fleur

Instagram: @chroniclesoffleur

Facebook: Help for Fleur

Fleur continues to thrive and as An Ambassador for Dogs supports Lucy's Law encouraging dogs to ask their owners to sign a petition to take dogs out of the hands of pet shops and dealers.

Fleur Supports #LucysLaw

Fleur also Supports #FinnsLaw

As no dog in any country deserves to be treated cruelly.

#happyeverafter

Illustrations by Alison Rumbles & Tony Colligan

Fleur

A Furry Tail

This is based on a true story of a dog called Fleur, who was rescued. A dog not ready to give up.

Follow her journey of discovery and remember if you really want something just don't give up

Once upon a time there was a little dog who was as white as snow walking the streets of Romania. She did not belong to anybody. She did not have a family. She had to search for food, she was trying to stay away from the other dogs and humans – playing hide and seek, keeping away from trouble.

One night the snow was falling all around her. She was cold and very hungry. Up until that night she was hard to see when the white snow laid on the floor, however now she was yellow and dirty. She was no longer camouflaged.

Turning a corner before she could run for her life, a net was tossed over her weak body and she was whipped off her feet.

The frightened little dog was captured, thrown into a van and then complete darkness surrounded her.

The little dog woke up shivering - she found herself in a rusty cage laid on a damp pallet. Snow was still falling heavily around her. She quickly realised that she was unable to move as there was a pain as sharp as a dagger.

She began to whimper and panic. An older dog in the next cage, spoke quietly, ''Pray to be saved little one, try to keep quiet''. The little dog could not move but continued to cry silently. The older dog continued to explain, ''If you are quiet you might get chosen to be rehomed if you're lucky. But make too much noise and they will not take you".

“Who will take me?” she asked,

“The Angels will come and take you – trust me I have been here a long time and I have seen so many young dogs come and go - they are the rescuers”.

The little dog drifted in and out of sleep. Dreaming of Angels coming to rescue her.

Suddenly a flashing light appeared that blinded her, and briefly took the pain away from her tummy, instead piercing her dark sunken eyes.

"What was that?" she thought, but could not make it out at first, something in the distance something not real.

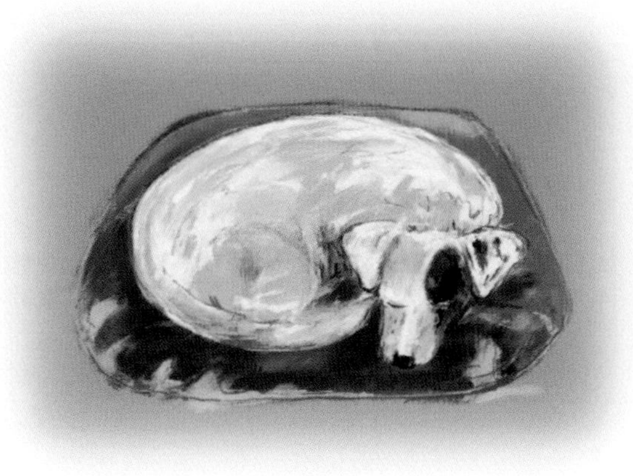

A vision all blurry

Was it an Angel like the older dog had said?

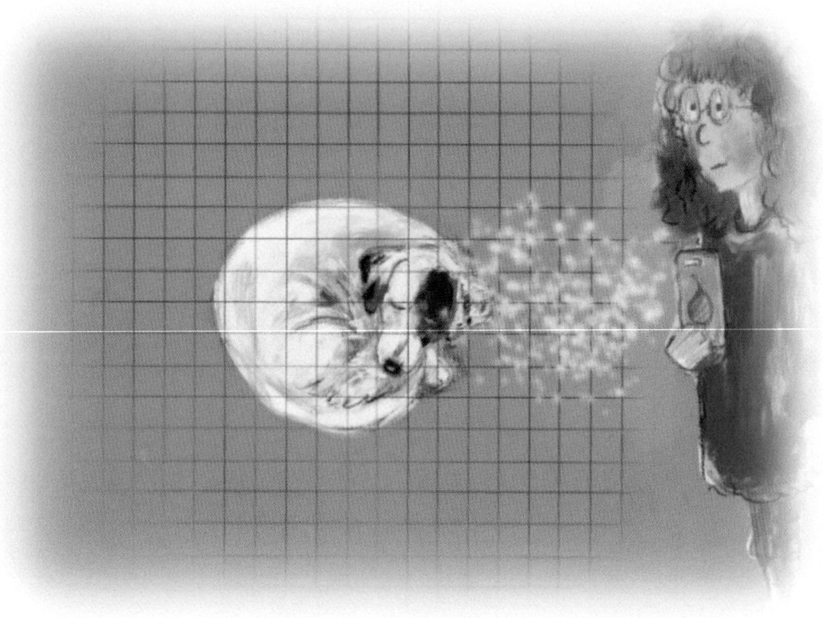

Or just a dream?

It was - an Angel called Eugenia.

She whispered, “Do not worry little dog, where there is life there is hope”.

The bright shining flashing light was her camera. The little dog drifted back into sleep hoping that it was an Angel sent to protect her whilst she slept.

The Angel had taken the little dog's photograph to share it on the internet.
Hoping someone will see this little dog and save her.

It had finally stopped snowing. Every night the little dog felt alone for every moment she was in pain, she was starting to lose hope. Feeling very weak and hungry the dog believed she saw a flutter of more snow, or was it?

No - it was not snow, it was feathers drifting down from the sky.

She imagined it was the Angel with the flashing light,
come to take her away so they could live happier ever after.

She was not wrong, there stood above her was not one, but two new Angels.

“Don’t be afraid little one, believe and trust in us”, said their sweet voices. The little dog saw a warm glow, smelt a sweet scent and felt loving arms around her.

The little dog was lifted gently, she felt safe, but then the sharp pain came back. The little dog became afraid and lashed out to the first Angel called Ramona – biting her hand.

Ramona realised the frail little dog was in trouble, that she was hurting and very unwell.

The second Angel called Alina wanted to help the little dog. She spoke quietly into the little dog's spotty ear, "you have a beautiful heart you have suffered a lot of pain, its ok little one we are here to help you now".

And so, between the two Angels they took the little dog and saved her in more ways than one.

Both the Angels loved her, fed her and nursed her back to health. The pain she was in before was due to an operation - to stop her from having puppies - which went horribly wrong. It left her tummy open to infection.

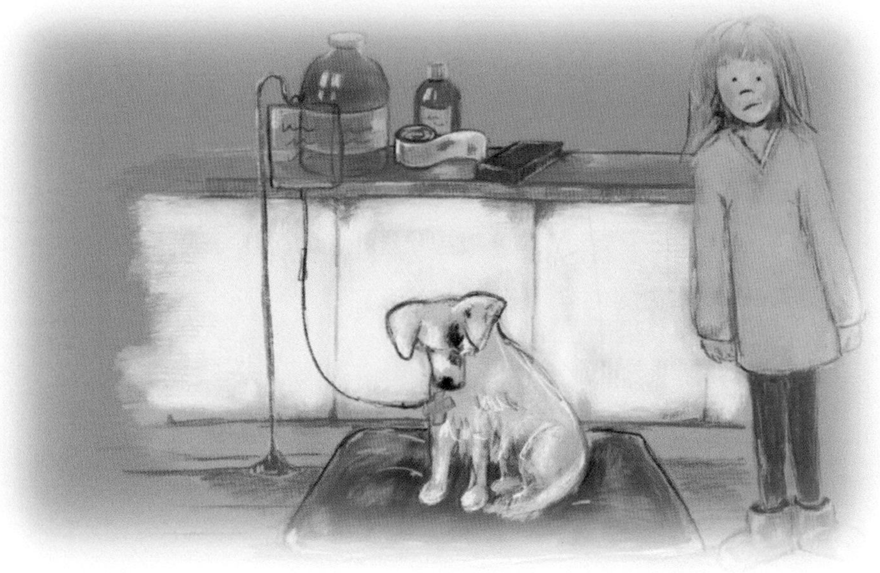

The Angels repaired her tummy and nursed her through the infections and fevers.

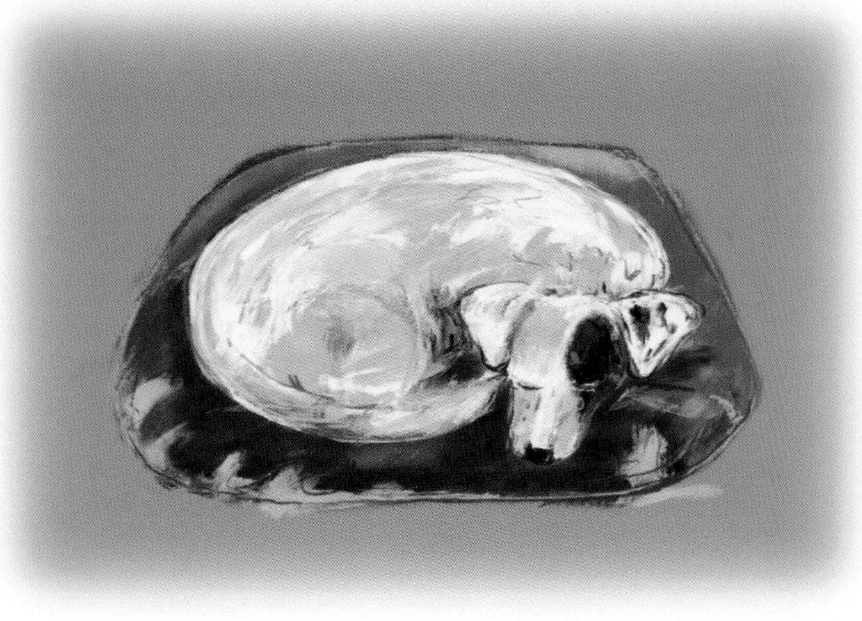

The little dog was very poorly with sepsis and was very sad.

As time passed the little dog blossomed.

The Angels called her Fleur, Fleur meaning flower in French.

It was time for the Angels to let Fleur find a loving home, they called upon a Rescue Angel who lived in England. This Angel was called Val and she was asked to help Fleur find her forever home.

Val was happy to help and posted a photograph on her website asking for Fleur to be adopted. It wasn't long before Fleurs picture was on a computer. The Morris Family saw this and asked to adopt her.

Fleur was now a beautiful white dog, who was gentle like the Angels.

Val said yes to the Morris Family to giving Fleur a forever after home.

Papa Morris and Mama Morris lived with their children Lisa, Michelle, Kim, Grant and Dannii who all lived together at Morris Manor. They had two very happy collie dogs one called Nero, one called Marti and a little foster dog called Maggsie. It was time for Fleur to be rehomed and be loved.

Fleur learned to play and fitted in very quickly with the Morris Family.

She enjoyed playing with Nero and Marti.

Sadly, three weeks into her new life Fleur collapsed in pain.

The pain again in her abdomen was extreme and it made her very sick. Papa Morris took Fleur to visit a vet. They had to operate immediately to save her life. Her body was infected again.

They had to remove a large part of her intestines, but still she remained very poorly. Fleur was now critically ill and again was needing special help, she needed a miracle.

The Angel Val was called upon to sprinkle her purple magic fairy dust to rescue Fleur once more. Through a plea for help and the power of social media, hope was found again.

Fleur was taken to a specialist hospital for pets where she had major surgery. It was the Royal Veterinary College Hospital.

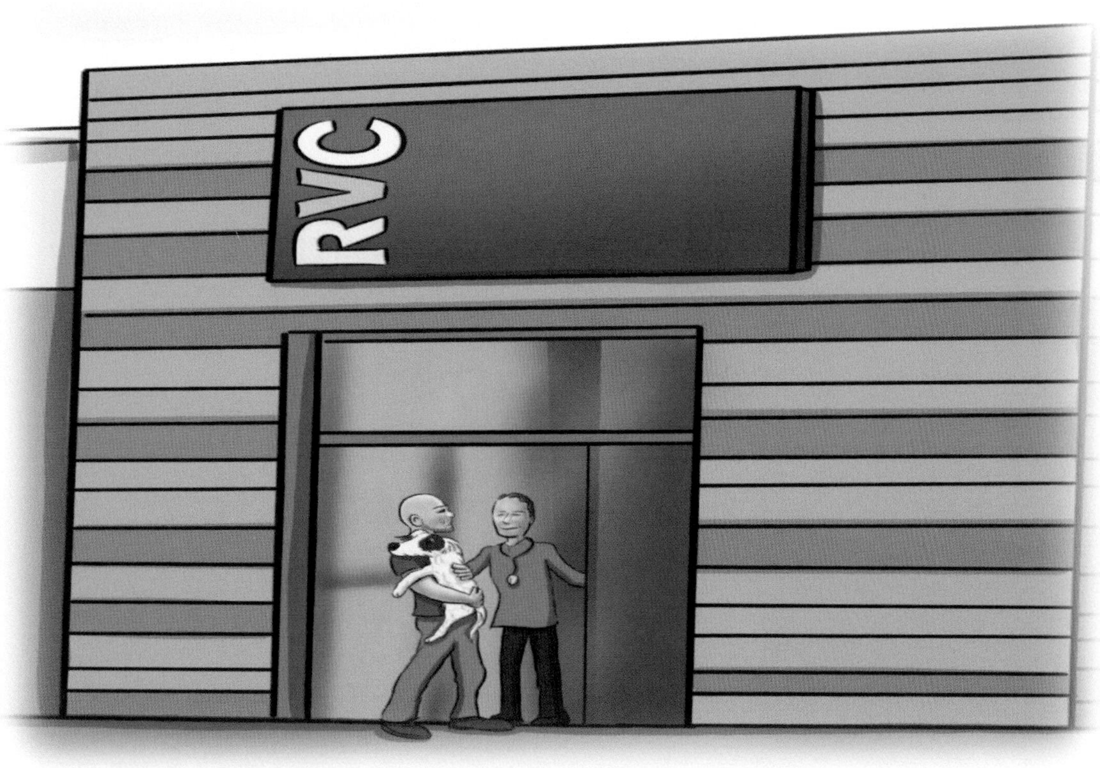

With the love of the nation, and care of specialist vets she recovered once more. She had to have major surgery, and lots of special nursing. She had a terrible infection and had sepsis.

Fleur was a miracle dog - from walking the poor streets of Romania, braving a life-threatening illness sepsis, to finding Papa and Mama Morris.

It was time to share Fleurs Story.

Mama Morris entered Fleur into a competition called Scruffs the nations favourite crossbreed competition.

Fleur won Scruffts Best Rescue 2017 and had become a finalist.

The next adventure was attending Crufts walking in the main arena of the world's biggest dog show.

Fleur walked with her head held high and swished her fluffy furry tail.

Fleur had become a beautiful flower, a princess, and an ambassador for rescue dogs.

From a single flashing camera in the shelter.

To the flashing lights and camera action of the Crufts, the world's greatest dog show.

Fleur was now the happiest dog in the world.

A true winner in life.

Fleur lives happily ever after, in her forever after home, touching the hearts of everyone she meets.

Living life to the full a winner in life Fleur a true survivor who never gave up.

Fleur passed an assessment to become a Pets at Therapy Dog.
Where she can go into schools and be a Read2Dog.
Helping children to read and communicate.

happy ever after

Follow Fleurs new adventures

Coming soon - the full true story

"A dog not ready to die……The Chronicles of Fleur"

New Titles

Just ask Sepsis

Common Cold

Visiting the Doctors Surgery

Fostering to Adoption Maggsie & Fleur

27756988R00022

Printed in Great Britain
by Amazon